CRYSTAL CLEAR

CRYSTAL CLEAR

A beginner's guide to

WORKING WITH STONES

BY NADIA BAILEY

ILLUSTRATED BY
MAYA BEUS

Smith
Street
Books

INTRODUCTION

WHAT IS A CRYSTAL?

The simplest definition is a solid mineral enclosed by symmetrically arranged planes, chosen for its durability and beauty, often cut and polished to bring out its unique characteristics. Yet this hardly sums up crystals' beauty and mysterious allure.

Humans have been drawn to these "flowers of the underworld" from our very earliest times. All over the world, our ancient ancestors fashioned stones and crystals into decorative objects, used them as practical tools, and placed them in burial grounds to honor their dead. They linked them to myths and stories about gods and heroes and ascribed them magical properties.

Today, crystals and stones still fascinate. Some people love them for their aesthetic appeal. Some are fascinated by the science of mineralogy. Some see them as spiritual tools, able to influence our mindset and emotions or connect us to the healing energies of the Earth and the universe.

However they're used, crystals form deep in the Earth over many millions of years as minerals are subjected to extreme temperature, pressure, and other geological forces. Most crystals are colorless in their pure state, but over the course of their creation, they integrate trace elements of other minerals. These "impurities" result in the stones' colors – for example, when iron and titanium are integrated into the colorless corundum, a blue sapphire forms; if chromium is introduced, it results in a ruby. Other stones require contact with water to form: turquoise, azurite, and malachite all receive their beautiful blue or green color from copper introduced by water.

Once formed, crystals make their way to us by a variety of means: many are mined, while some are spontaneously brought to the Earth's surface via upheavals like volcanic eruptions, others discovered in the ocean.

But some popular crystals aren't crystals at all: while they're sold in the same stores and used for the same purposes as stones like amethyst and citrine, they don't belong to the same scientific category. For example, agate may have the outward appearance of a gemstone, but it lacks a crystalline structure – this makes it a mineraloid rather than a true mineral. Others like pearl, jet, ammonite, and amber aren't stones at all, but organic materials that were created by living organisms.

Crystals, stone or otherwise, are a large category and can be classified in many different ways – by their species (for example, beryl, corundum, chalcedony, feldspar, quartz, or tourmaline), their crystalline structure (cubic, tetragonal, hexagonal, trigonal, orthorhombic, monoclinic, or triclinic), their hardness, their luster, and more. If a crystal has a rough finish, uneven edges, and multiple points, it is most likely a raw crystal; these may have one or more flat, shiny surfaces, but for the most part they have an untreated, natural look as though they were just unearthed. If a stone is shiny and polished all over, with a smooth, glossy surface, it is likely a tumbled gemstone that has undergone a variety of possible techniques to bring out its beauty. Other stones may be cut, faceted, or carved, especially if they're destined for jewelry. These processes bring out a stone's unique characteristics, such as luster, clarity, or color; it's worth noting that not all stones on the market get their color naturally – most amethysts, for example, are heat-treated to bring out their vibrant hue, while emeralds and rubies are bathed in warmed oil. Other stones may be bleached or dyed to enhance or change their colors. If you wish to avoid crystals that have been treated, consult your seller, who will be able to advise you.

Starting a collection of crystals can be daunting for the beginner. It's wise to do some research on the many different kinds available, paying attention to their qualities, associations, and uses, as well as factors like rarity and price. You don't need to spend a great deal of money to start a collection – while precious stones like diamonds, rubies, and emeralds might be out of reach, stones like clear quartz, carnelian, and chrysoprase are widely available and can be purchased at a variety of price points. Often, the best way to start a collection is to let a stone pick you, simply by paying attention to which resonates most strongly when held in your hand. Let your intuition guide you.

'All over the world, our ancient ancestors fashioned stones and crystals into decorative objects, used them as practical tools, and placed them in burial grounds to honor their dead.'

CRYSTAL CARE

Different gems require different treatment, and best practices for storing, cleaning, and display can vary from stone to stone. Most respond well to warm water, mild detergent, and a gentle polish with a soft cloth. However, some gems have specific sensitivities. For example, while some stones benefit from exposure to sunlight, stones like amethyst, aquamarine, citrine, and opal will fade or crack if exposed to too much heat. Some stones prefer a dark environment (such as a closed box, velvet bag, or – as ancient lore suggests – a black silk handkerchief) to maintain their hue and properties, while others must be regularly worn against the skin to be at their best. Be mindful of how you handle gemstones as some species are fragile and will shatter if treated roughly. Gemstones such as lapis lazuli, turquoise, malachite, and pearl are particularly sensitive to acids, perfumes, detergents, soaps, and other liquids, and special care must be taken with them. Your crystal seller will be able to advise on how to care for different types of stones.

CRYSTAL CLEANSING AND CHARGING

In the medieval tradition, a gemstone could be charged by anointing it with the name of a saint and the sign of the Cross in olive oil, turning to the east, placing it in the hands of a baptized child, and then praying until the saint appeared in the face of the stone. These days, simpler methods are preferred: place your crystals in sunlight for a brief period to energize them or cover them in soil and leave overnight. To cleanse your stones, submerge them in salt or running water, smudge them with smoke, or leave them in the path of the moon so that they are bathed in its lunar light. Crystals can also be cleansed and rejuvenated by placing them in proximity to clear quartz, selenite, or jet. Be sure to check the particular needs of your gemstone variety before cleansing and charging, as some require special care.

'To cleanse your stones, submerge them in salt or running water, smudge them with smoke, or leave them in the path of the moon so that they are bathed in its lunar light.'

ETHICAL SOURCING

Currently, there is no worldwide standard or certification for ethical crystals – this means the industry is largely unregulated and there is little transparency around the working conditions of miners and the complex supply chains that bring crystals from the Earth to you. The people who do the hard work of unearthing these stones are often low-paid laborers. The work is dangerous, often carried out underground – miners may face landslides or rock falls. They also face the threat of silicosis, caused by fine dust and quartz particles that penetrate deep into the lungs. In many countries where minerals are mined, child labor is widespread.

As a conscious consumer, always seek retailers who are open and honest about where their crystals come from, including transparency about a crystal's origins, the mine it was sourced from, the working conditions of laborers, and the route the crystal took to arrive in their store. Be wary of retailers who lack information about where and how their stones are mined or who sell their stones at too-good-to-be-true prices. Not all crystal sellers are committed to providing ethically sourced gems: some do the hard work to establish relationships with suppliers who live up to the kind of standards you would expect – but others source from companies with poor environmental records and histories of labor violations. If in doubt, ask questions. If a seller isn't transparent about their sourcing policies, you should take your business elsewhere. Don't be afraid to shop around until you find a seller whose ethical practices are as attractive as their gems.

LAB-GROWN OR NATURAL?

While the crystals of antiquity all came from the Earth, today many specimens are created through scientific means. While it's difficult to spot the difference based on appearance alone, you may prefer one type to the other. Many people who are interested in the metaphysical side of crystals believe that natural stones are superior, imbued with the energy of their creation. However, natural crystals are sourced by mining, something with an environmental and human impact. If these considerations are important to you, you may want to consider cultured (that is, lab-grown) stones as an alternative.

These days, it's possible to grow rocks that have the same physical, chemical, and optical characteristics as their natural counterparts: stones that don't need to be mined in unsafe conditions and that have a lesser environmental impact. That said, you can still make sustainability a priority whether you opt for natural or lab-grown crystals – it's a matter of choosing well, buying less, and considering shopping second hand. Instead of collecting masses of gems, try cultivating a small collection that truly resonates with you.

'Instead of collecting masses of gems, try cultivating a small collection of stones that truly resonates with you.'

USING CRYSTALS

There are many ways that people integrate crystals into their lives and routines. For some, crystals are primarily aesthetic objects, which may be displayed in special cases or simply placed throughout the home; you might experiment by using crystals as part of a vignette with other special objects, organizing them by color for a pretty tonal effect.

Crystals can lend a calming energy, making them perfect for creating a spa-like atmosphere in the bathroom. A couple of crystals placed in a nook of the shower can add a touch of romance to your bathing ritual – an amethyst or rose quartz is ideal for this purpose.

Crystals can also aid in activities like yoga – try matching a stimulating vinyasa flow with an energizing stone like citrine or rutilated quartz, or complement a soothing yin practice with chalcedony or moonstone. A heart-opening practice could benefit from the influence of a chrysoprase or emerald, while the effects of a grounding practice could be amplified by keeping a piece of agate or jasper close by. Crystals can also aid in meditation – by gazing at a beautiful stone, you might find that centering and focusing the mind come more easily. A calming stone like iolite, moonstone, or labradorite would be ideal for this purpose.

Many people like to use crystals as talismans or amulets, either worn as a piece of jewelry, placed on a workstation or bedside table, or simply carried close to the body in a bag or pocket. You can pick different stones to keep close by choosing what kind of energy you want to shift, amplify, or attract. A piece of dioptase kept on your desk could lend a sense of tranquility, helping to balance out the stress of the office. The lunar glow of some selenite by your bedside could help the transition to a peaceful mindset before you go to bed. A black onyx carried in your pocket might act as a reminder that you are strong and capable during a challenging time. Setting clear intentions and showing up for yourself is usually the best mindset to approach this kind of application.

How you use your crystals will be unique and individual to you. Tap into your intuition, let your inner voice guide you, and know that you are your own best teacher. In the meantime, this book will help you on your path.

CRYSTALS

AGATE

A stone of stability and protection that connects us to the grounding influence of the Earth.

PHYSICAL PROPERTIES

A variety of chalcedony, this distinctly banded stone appears in a wide variety of patterns and hues – its diversity of appearance is perhaps its most distinctive quality. Ordinary agate is banded, but when the stone exhibits branching, plant-like patterns, it is known as moss agate. Agate can be opaque, waxy, translucent, or almost transparent.

HISTORY AND LORE

Agate's name is derived from the river Achates in Sicily, where it was discovered. Its earliest mention in literature is in the treatise *On Stones* by Theophrastus, a philosopher and contemporary of Aristotle; he refers to it as a beautiful stone sold at a high price.

In the ancient world around the Mediterranean, agate was believed to have a cooling influence on the body and was used to ward off fever and disease. It was a prized gemstone for amulets, carved seals, signets, and rings; many stones were engraved with magical inscriptions to heighten their powers. During the Middle Ages, agate was made into drinking cups as it was believed to counter the effect of poison.

Germany, Brazil, Uruguay, India, and Mexico are the best sources of banded agates, although they are found all over the world.

STRENGTHS

Agate is a protective stone that helps fortify the body and spirit, enhancing positive energy. Agate inspires self-confidence and eases stress in times of pressure – place a piece of agate in your workspace to keep you centered no matter what the day brings. With its grounding, stabilizing energy, it can be used as a talisman to enhance grace, bring balance, and promote harmony.

Gemini

Mercury

May

Base

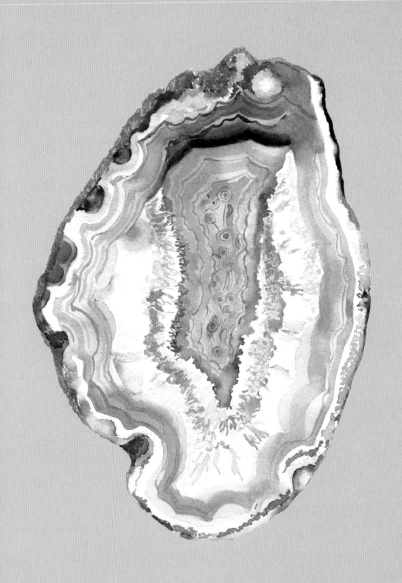

ALEXANDRITE

One of nature's most unique stones, alexandrite reminds us that our natural state is one of balance.

PHYSICAL PROPERTIES

Alexandrite has marked hues of red and green; by daylight it is bright or emerald green, but in artificial light, it transforms to a soft red. Part of the chrysoberyl family, alexandrite is known as a phenomenal gem, meaning it changes color or shifts and transforms depending on the light. Other phenomenal stones include moonstone, cat's-eye, opal, and labradorite. Due to alexandrite's scarcity, the stone is highly prized.

HISTORY AND LORE

Gemini and Aquarius

Alexandrite was discovered in 1834 in the Ural's emerald mines on Prince Alexander II's sixteenth birthday; the stone was named in honor of the future Russian ruler. Because alexandrite's red and green hues matched the country's military colors, it became one of the most prized gemstones among the Russian aristocracy.

Outside of Russia, alexandrite has also been discovered in Sri Lanka, Myanmar, Zimbabwe, Zambia, and Brazil.

Mercury

STRENGTHS

June

With its chameleonic quality, alexandrite symbolizes hope, prosperity, calm, and fertility, as well as energy, activity, self-expression, and power. In its daylight aspect, it corresponds to luck and good fortune, while at night, it unites the heart and body, stimulating love and passion. Alexandrite reminds us of the duality that exists within ourselves and helps us integrate opposing aspects. It is especially powerful for those who want to develop their creativity or foster the ability to embrace change and flexibility. Use one as part of your meditation practice to tap into your creative intuition. Alexandrite is considered a lucky stone for those born on a Friday.

Crown

AMBER

Recalling golden sunlight, this
beautiful resin invites self-expression
and wards off negative influences.

PHYSICAL PROPERTIES

Ranges from an almost completely transparent light yellow to red-
orange to dark brown, with a resinous or waxy luster. Neither a gem
nor a mineral, amber is the fossilized resin of trees, transformed
by heat and pressure over millions of years. One of its most unique
aspects is that it may contain elements of plant matter or insects,
such as mosquitos, suspended within.

HISTORY AND LORE

Amber can be found all over the world, but is historically
associated with the Baltic region, where it is particularly prized.
It takes its name from the word *anbar*, which means "perfume"
in Arabic, because of its resinous odor.

Taurus

In Greek mythology, amber was formed from tears shed by the
Electrides on news of their brother Phaeton's death. The nymphs
transformed into poplar trees and their perpetual tears became
amber. Other origin myths include the belief that it was the tears
of a sea bird or honey melted by the sun and solidified by the
sea. In ancient China, it was believed that amber was formed
by the souls of tigers upon their release from this plane.

Sun and
Saturn

STRENGTHS

November

Amber is a stone of positivity and optimism, encouraging the
flow of good energy in both the body and the home. It banishes
negative influences and promotes intuition. Resonating with the
solar plexus, amber relates to the material world and promotes
good fortune, success, and gains on all material levels. Keep
a piece of amber in your wallet to promote a mindful attitude
toward your finances. Amber can also be used as a tool to aid in
self-healing – it helps turn painful experiences into opportunities
for transformation.

Solar Plexus

AMETHYST

A purifying and amplifying stone renowned for its spiritual energy and captivating purple shade.

PHYSICAL PROPERTIES

Iconically purple, amethyst is a variety of crystalline quartz known for its hardness and durability. It can fall anywhere from the lightest violet tinge to the deep velvety hue of red wine.

HISTORY AND LORE

Its name comes from the Greek *amethystos*, meaning "without drunkenness"; a Greek myth tells how a nymph, pursued by the god Dionysus, transformed into a crystal to escape his unwelcome attentions. The god bestowed the stone with the color of his sacred wine, vowing that whoever wore an amethyst would be safe from intoxication, no matter how much they drank.

Aries and Pisces

At one time it was known as the "bishop's stone" because of its popularity with the early Catholic clergy, and is said to be the favorite gem of Saint Valentine.

Amethyst occurs in many locations around the world, with Brazil known for its abundance of high-quality stones.

Jupiter

STRENGTHS

Amethyst is considered one of the most powerful crystals. It is a stone for lovers, creatives, and pioneers, promoting connectivity, spirituality, passion, and original thought, as well as temperance and sobriety. Amethyst puts us in touch with the mental world, which makes it a stone of focused thought – perfect for meditation, transformation, and assimilating new knowledge. A stone of alignment, it can help harmonize the mental, physical, emotional, and spiritual realms. Kept by the bedside, amethyst invites rest and promotes a peaceful environment. Put a stone under your pillow to invite visions and dreams. Especially lucky worn on a Thursday.

February

Crown

AMMONITE

A grounding and protective stone which promotes stability and structure.

PHYSICAL PROPERTIES

The fossils of extinct ocean-dwelling mollusks, ammonites have a distinctive spiral shape resembling a ram's horn. Some display iridescence – when found in clays, their original mother-of-pearl coating is often preserved.

HISTORY AND LORE

Found nearly everywhere on the planet where oceans previously existed, ammonites were once believed to be snakes miraculously turned into stone by saints; in medieval Europe, ammonites were known as "snake stones" or "serpent stones."

The ancient Roman writer and natural philosopher Pliny the Elder called them *ammonis cornua* (horns of Ammon), after the Egyptian god Ammon (also known as Amun), who was usually represented with ram's horns – the origin of ammonite's modern name.

A particular species of ammonite native to northern Nepal is considered sacred by adherents of Hinduism, Buddhism, and followers of the Himalayan religion Bon. Known as shaligrams, these ammonite stones are forged by the landscape over millennia and are believed to possess their own intrinsic consciousness. Shaligrams are kept in homes and temples, regarded as both living gods and active members of the community.

STRENGTHS

Ammonite is symbolic of change and evolution. It offers physical and spiritual grounding and invites connection to all living things. Its distinctive spiral shape draws in and filters negative energy, releasing it as fresh, positive energy, which cleanses the soul and promotes personal growth. Use ammonite as a meditation tool for spiraling into the center of your consciousness, your heart, and your spiritual core. This stone encourages us to reflect on our patterns of behavior without judgement, encouraging growth and transformation.

Aries

Mars and Jupiter

March and April

Root

AQUAMARINE

A radiant stone that reminds us
of the lightness of air, the blue of
the sky, and the beauty of the ocean.

PHYSICAL PROPERTIES

A variety of beryl, aquamarine ranges from clear sky blue to a
bluish-green, with a vitreous luster. Most aquamarine is very light in
color, while those with a rich hue are the rarest and most valuable.

HISTORY AND LORE

With a name recalling the sea (from the Latin *aqua marina*,
meaning "sea water") aquamarine was historically believed to have
a refreshing influence by the West, its colors recalling the calming
hues of the ocean, fields, and trees. Once thought to form from the
tears of sea nymphs, another legend suggested it was the treasure
of mermaids. Due to its ongoing association with the ocean, it is
considered a favored stone for sailors and anyone traveling at sea.

To the early Christians, aquamarine offered protection from
evil spirits – if you held one in your mouth, you might safely
call a demon out of hell to answer your questions. During the
Renaissance, it was known as the "sweet tempered stone."

Brazil has been the world's leading source of gem-quality
aquamarine for over 100 years, but it is found everywhere from
Nigeria to Pakistan to Sri Lanka.

STRENGTHS

A calming, soothing, and cleansing stone, aquamarine inspires
deep thought, tranquility, peace, and surrender. It releases stress
and promotes inner calm, clearing the consciousness and releasing
negative emotions. Use aquamarine to gain awareness and
clarity about your own emotions, and to heighten your sensitivity
to others' feelings. Aquamarine helps us move through life with
more ease, on journeys both physical and spiritual – a good stone
to keep close when traveling.

Scorpio

Saturn and
Neptune

March and
October

Throat

BLACK ONYX

A stone of endurance that aids in meeting challenges and overcoming psychic blocks.

PHYSICAL PROPERTIES

An opaque black stone, most often featuring dark and light parallel bands, with a dull luster and waxy texture. It is a variety of chalcedony.

HISTORY AND LORE

Capricorn

The word onyx comes from the Greek *onux*, meaning "fingernail," because the stone was thought to resemble the luster and appearance of a fingernail. In antiquity, onyx was believed to have a disquieting effect, imparting prophetic and bewildering dreams, which could only be tempered by wearing sardonyx at the same time.

Saturn

The ancient Egyptians believed that an onyx worn around the neck would cool and temper the ardors of love. Christians in the Middle Ages prized rosaries made of the stone, which were thought to aid in concentration and devotion.

Onyx is found in many regions throughout the world.

July

STRENGTHS

Root

Carry an onyx when you need some extra psychic armor, whether you're facing a conflict or adventuring into strange places. Onyx encourages emotional equilibrium, aids spiritual inspiration, and helps to balance excessive emotions. An especially useful stone for gaining focus, thinking objectively, and warding off negative thoughts. Place one at your workstation to encourage mental endurance and grounding.

BLOODSTONE

A stone of courage and strength that provides a mental boost when motivation is lacking.

PHYSICAL PROPERTIES

An opaque dark green stone flecked with blood-red spots, with a waxy, resinous luster. Bloodstone is a variety of chalcedony – its distinctive red spots are caused by the presence of iron oxide.

HISTORY AND LORE

Bloodstone is also known as heliotrope, which means "sun turner" in Greek. In antiquity, it was said that bloodstone placed in water gave it a reddish tint, and when the sun struck that water, the reflections would shine a brilliant red.

Aries

The ancient Greeks thought the stone had fallen from the heavens, while the Romans believed it had the power to stop wounds from bleeding. Bloodstone, as recorded by Pliny the Elder, could be used as a mirror to observe solar eclipses.

During ancient Roman times around the Mediterranean, it was said that the stone's distinctive coloring was reminiscent of the red glow of the sun setting over the deep green sea.

Mercury

Known as the "martyr's stone" in medieval Europe, early Christians believed that its red markings appeared when a piece lay at the foot of the cross on which Christ was crucified.

The most significant deposits of bloodstone are found in India, Australia, Brazil, China, and the United States.

March

STRENGTHS

The bloodstone enhances courage and provides clarity during times of uncertainty or indecision. It invites faithfulness, patience, and organization: a good stone to keep close when you are working on a new idea or bringing a project to fruition. The bloodstone bolsters inner strength and promotes wisdom, a calm mind, and resilience. Especially lucky worn on a Tuesday.

Root

CARNELIAN

Both invigorating and balancing, the carnelian is a stone of vitality and creativity.

PHYSICAL PROPERTIES

Translucent to opaque, the carnelian is a form of chalcedony ranging from a pale orange to a deep red. Its distinctive red hue is caused by the presence of iron during the stone's formation.

HISTORY AND LORE

Carnelian takes its name from the Latin *carneus*, meaning flesh colored. Like bloodstone, it was sometimes known as the "martyr's stone."

Taurus, Leo, and Virgo

To the ancient Egyptians, carnelian symbolized rebirth and was believed to aid the deceased in the next world – for this reason, it was commonly placed in tombs and used as votive offerings.

The stone was particularly important to the shamans of Siberia and Tartary, who prized it as a talisman against disease. In the nineteenth century, practitioners of Theosophy believed that carnelian bestowed the power to view the astral plane if steadily gazed upon.

Mars

Major sources of carnelian include Brazil, India, and Uruguay, but it is mined worldwide.

July and August

STRENGTHS

Carnelian is a stone of stability: it promotes peaceful thoughts, helps to calm anger, and brings steadiness during times of transition. Known for replacing negative energy with positive, it encourages inner strength and enhances harmony, dignity, and power. This stone aids in reaching goals and promoting creativity and self-worth – carry one in your pocket whenever you need to tap into these energies. It is especially lucky when worn on a Sunday.

Sacral

CAT'S-EYE

A rare and beautiful stone known to attract abundance and invite wealth in all forms.

PHYSICAL PROPERTIES

A semi-transparent variety of chrysoberyl which displays a distinctive ray of light on its surface known as chatoyancy. This stone is usually seen in shades of yellow or green. These stones are rare and are consequently highly prized.

HISTORY AND LORE

Gemini
and Leo

Named for its resemblance to the enigmatic gaze of a feline, cat's-eye is also known as cymophane; the latter is derived from the Greek for "appear" and "wave," referring to the movement of light within the stone. The ancient Romans connected it to the sun and fire, calling it *oculus solis*, or "eye of the sun."

Ancient Mesopotamians believed cat's-eye made the wearer invisible in battle, while other superstitions held that a spirit or genie, trapped inside the stone, gave it its captivating appearance.

Sun, Mercury,
Venus, Mars,
and Pluto

Regarded as lucky when it comes to wealth, the stone was a popular charm throughout history for success in speculation, gambling, and games of chance. It became fashionable in Europe in the late nineteenth century after Princess Louise Margaret of Prussia wore a cat's-eye ring following her wedding to Prince Arthur, Duke of Connaught and Strathearn.

Sri Lanka is known as a source of high-quality stones.

June and
November

STRENGTHS

Cat's-eye is a balancing stone, enhancing wisdom and inviting prosperity. It attracts abundance in all forms, promoting spiritual and creative wealth as well as material gain. Endowing clarity, cat's-eye can help you think clearly before you act. This gemstone fosters optimism and renewal, and is especially lucky when worn on a Thursday.

Solar Plexus

CHALCEDONY

With its soothing influence, chalcedony is a stone for support during times of emotional upheaval.

PHYSICAL PROPERTIES

Usually white, gray, and pale blue–gray, with a waxy luster. Stones with strong color saturation and high translucence are the most sought after.

HISTORY AND LORE

This stone either takes its name from the city of Chalcedon in Bithynia, historically known for its deposits of copper, now a district of Istanbul named Kadıköy, or from Karchedon, the Greek name for the North African port city of Carthage, through which it was transported during the seventeenth century.

Cancer

In ancient Greece, chalcedony was associated with the weather, used to ward off disorders caused by changes in atmosphere and the seasons. Among soldiers, it was associated with victory.

In Italy, white chalcedony is known as *pietra lattea*, meaning "milky stone," and was long believed to increase the supply of milk in breastfeeding mothers. Chalcedony was considered sacred to Diana in ancient Rome. In the Middle Ages, it was thought to drive away visions of ghosts. The Rosicrucians saw it as a symbol of divine victory.

Moon

Chalcedony is found throughout the world, including Brazil, India, Australia, and the United States.

May and June

STRENGTHS

Chalcedony supports both physical and emotional fortitude, teaching us that true strength lies in vulnerability. It protects against melancholy and lethargy, and invites emotional stability and devotion – try wearing it close to the heart to tap into these qualities. With its calm strength and gentle energy, chalcedony connect us to a feminine energy, quelling restlessness and impatience. A powerful stone for those ruled by the moon.

Throat

CHRYSOPRASE

A stone to bring about healing and serenity, which especially resonates with matters of the heart.

PHYSICAL PROPERTIES

An apple-green stone, sometimes likened to moonlight's tender hue, with a greasy or waxy luster. Chrysoprase is one of the most sought-after varieties of chalcedony.

HISTORY AND LORE

Cancer and
Pisces

The ancient Greeks believed that if chrysoprase came into contact with poison, it would lose its color. According to an ancient Eastern European legend, it could grant the wearer the power to understand the language of animals, while the early Christians saw it as a stone of martyrs, representing divine sacrifice.

Due to its verdant color, the stone has historical associations with renewal and spring, the time when nature comes back to life after the long winter.

Moon and
Venus

Substantial deposits of the stone were discovered in Silesia in the fourteenth century, which were subsequently used to decorate the chapel of Saint Wenceslas in Prague's St Vitus Cathedral.

Chrysoprase has been found throughout Eastern Europe, as well as Australia, Brazil, Kazakhstan, Myanmar, and Tanzania.

May

STRENGTHS

Chrysoprase offers a purifying and healing influence and invites compassion towards the self and others. It stimulates creativity and the imagination and helps calm the mind. Like other green stones, it is associated with love and is known for promoting optimism, empathy, and emotional balance. Placed under the pillow or by the bedside, it can impart a calming influence on the tired and sick of heart. Chrysoprase is considered a lucky stone for those ruled by the moon and for anyone born during spring.

Heart

CITRINE

An energizing stone to clear stagnant energy and bring about optimism and joy.

PHYSICAL PROPERTIES

A clear, light yellow or orange quartz with a vitreous luster. Unlike many kinds of quartz, naturally occurring citrine is rare; to produce the stone, other varieties of quartz such as amethyst are dyed or heat-treated.

HISTORY AND LORE

Leo and
Scorpio

Citrine takes its name from its citron tint. In the European Middle Ages, it was carried as a protective talisman against diseases and was believed to ward off evil thought forms. During this period, it signified fruitfulness, faithfulness, and love towards a higher power, and was thought to bring about miracles.

Citrine has been called the "golden stone of wealth" and the "merchant's stone" because it was believed to attract material abundance.

Virtually all natural citrines come from Brazil.

Sun and
Jupiter

STRENGTHS

November

Carrying the power of the sun, citrine is a stone of manifestation, creativity, and fortitude. It encourages protection, alignment, and energy, awakens the imagination, and transforms thought into action. Citrine promotes self-confidence and self-belief, and can amplify positive emotions; with its solar associations, it may help people whose energy and mood dip during winter months. It is a stone that enhances communication, whether at work, in personal relationships, or with the self. In situations that lack clarity, citrine illuminates the way forward. It is a fortunate stone for anyone ruled by the sun.

Solar plexus

CLEAR QUARTZ

The chameleon of the gem world, clear quartz is a transformative stone that transmutes energy.

PHYSICAL PROPERTIES

A pure and transparent variety of quartz with a vitreous luster – the clearest stones, free from feathers or inclusions, are highly prized. Colorless quartz is abundant, but exceptionally clear samples large enough to make crystal balls, bowls, or scrying glasses are very rare.

HISTORY AND LORE

Also known as rock crystal, clear quartz has been reputed to contain a universe unto itself within its prisms. Across the ancient world, it was believed to be frozen or fossilized water. For this reason, it was used in widespread rituals to promote rain and was thought to satisfy thirst if held in the mouth.

The ancient Meso-Americans believed that clear quartz held the power to reflect the past and future. Western European fortune tellers and psychics carved it into crystal balls and scrying glasses to receive visions and divine the causes of disease, a practice that appears to date back to the fifth century.

Dating to at least sixteenth century Germany, this stone was also called *schwindelstein*, or "vertigo stone," as it was thought to prevent dizziness. Other historical names include "god-stone" in ancient Ireland and "ice of eternity" in ancient Greece.

Clear quartz is found in Brazil, Japan, Madagascar, Australia, Canada, and the United States.

STRENGTHS

A stone of amplification, clear quartz magnifies the properties of other crystals in its vicinity. It absorbs negative energy and renders it harmless, while also releasing and enhancing positive energy. Clear quartz regulates thought and emotions and provides a stabilizing, cleansing influence.

Pisces

Sun, Mercury, Moon, and Uranus

April

Third Eye

CORAL

This gift from the sea vibrates
with active energy and stimulates
confidence and decisiveness.

PHYSICAL PROPERTIES

Generally pale pink to deep red in color. Although coral is naturally
matte, it can be polished to a glassy shine. Coral is not technically
a stone, but a secretion of calcium carbonate, produced by colonies
of plant-like animals called polyps.

HISTORY AND LORE

Cancer,
Scorpio, and
Pisces

In ancient Greece, coral was thought to have formed when the hero
Perseus slayed the sorceress Medusa – as her blood dripped into
the sea, it hardened and transformed into coral. In ancient Egypt,
coral was placed in tombs to protect the dead from evil spirits,
as it was believed that each piece contained the blood of the gods.

During the Middle Ages in France, it was used to make *pater de
sang* or blood rosary which were thought to stop hemorrhages,
while in Italy and elsewhere in Europe, coral has traditionally been
used to protect against the evil eye.

Venus and
Mars

Coral is found in reefs in warm, shallow seas, particularly east of
Australia, and around Japan, Africa, and the Mediterranean.

STRENGTHS

October

Coral aids confidence and courage. It enhances focus and
inspires action while guarding against lethargy and indecision.
Worn close to the body, it helps temper emotions and transform
chaotic energy, while offering support during periods of change
and transformation. Coral inspires hope and fosters connections,
especially to community. It is especially lucky when worn on a
Tuesday and for those ruled by Mars.

Root

DIAMOND

Representative of unparalleled strength and clarity, the diamond is a stone to value.

PHYSICAL PROPERTIES

Available in many colors, the most valuable diamonds are completely clear, with brilliant adamantine luster and a high refraction, reflection, and dispersion of light. Diamonds may occur in shades of yellow, green, pink, red, blue, gray, and black.

HISTORY AND LORE

Diamond's name originates with the Greek word *adamas*, meaning "unconquerable." Brilliant and resistant, it has been an emblem of fearlessness and invincibility from the ancient Greek era onward.

Aries, Leo, and Libra

Across the ancient world and into the recent past, the diamond was endowed with many powers – from curing insanity to protecting against poison – but legend tells that a diamond should be received as a gift or won, rather than purchased.

In ancient India, the diamond was known as the "invincible stone," and was considered a symbol of virtue and justice. During the European Middle Ages, diamonds were believed to protect against the plague; those with the means wore them to ward off the Black Death.

Sun

Africa has long been the center of diamond mining, but quality stones also come from Australia, Russia, Canada, and elsewhere. Today, diamonds are one of the most valuable stones.

April

STRENGTHS

Diamond is a gem of strength and fearlessness – it promotes inner courage and inspires meaningful action. It bestows a sense of self-confidence, enhances concentration, and heightens spiritual ecstasy. Diamond fosters love, trust, and commitment. Though commonly associated with romance, it also represents divine love. Due to its clarity and brilliance, it is the ideal object of contemplation to bring about deep and profound meditation.

All

CRYSTAL CLEAR

DIOPTASE

A heart-opening stone known for its sensitivity and brilliant green hue.

PHYSICAL PROPERTIES

A transparent green or blue-green crystal with a vitreous luster. Due to its brittleness, dioptase should always be handled and stored with care.

HISTORY AND LORE

An exceptionally rare stone, dioptase takes its name from the Greek *dia*, meaning "through," and *optomai*, meaning "to see."

Due to the intensity of its color, dioptase has a long history of use as a pigment in painting: it was one of the materials – along with ochre, carbon black, and lime white – used to decorate the famous Neolithic lime plaster statuettes of 'Ain Ghazal in Jordan, which date from the ninth century BCE.

Taurus

According to ancient lore, dioptase strengthened the sight of those who gazed on it – a quality shared by the emerald.

Venus

Dioptase is often found in arid regions, alongside copper deposits, with the best specimens coming from Kazakhstan, the United States, and throughout Africa.

STRENGTHS

May

Dioptase embodies compassion and forgiveness. It assists in quelling negative and destructive thought patterns, while encouraging positive shifts in perspective. Its powerful green hue invites us to become more sensitive and open to nature – try keeping a piece of dioptase in your living space to deepen your connection to the natural world. Use dioptase to overcome emotional struggles and stimulate renewal, and as a means to connect the emotional heart with the spiritual heart to receive abundance.

Heart

EMERALD

A radiant stone that opens the eyes to new possibilities and invites love in all its forms.

PHYSICAL PROPERTIES

A deep, saturated green stone, ranging from transparent to opaque. A variety of beryl, most emeralds are not entirely clear but contain inclusions called jardin ("garden" in French), because they resemble leaves and branches.

HISTORY AND LORE

Emerald takes its name from the Greek *smaragdos* for "green," which evolved into the Latin *smaragdus*, and eventually into the Middle English *emerallde*. The emerald was dedicated to Venus in Roman mythology and Hathor in the Egyptian tradition, both goddesses of love, and has been held as a fortunate stone for women since antiquity.

Taurus

The ancient Romans believed that an emerald would change from vivid green to dull brown if its wearer's lover was faithless. In the 1600s, the Flemish writer Anselmus de Boodt recorded that an emerald, unable to do its possessor good or to avert evil, would shiver into a thousand pieces, broken by despair.

Though emeralds are found throughout the world, the three main sources are in Colombia, Brazil, and Zambia.

Venus

STRENGTHS

May

Emerald is a stone of love and renewal. It embodies unity, promotes compassion, and inspires artistic creativity. Emerald invites receptivity, especially in romantic endeavors – wear it as a pendant or in a pocket close to the heart to amplify these qualities. Associated with the fertile energy of Venus, emerald opens the way to new beginnings – use it to focus your energy on a new project, usher in a new relationship, or to gain a new perspective. Emerald is especially lucky when worn on a Friday.

Heart

GARNET

A stone of vitality that awakens us to take action and embark on new endeavors.

PHYSICAL PROPERTIES

Typically a deep red stone similar in hue to a ruby, garnets can also be as green as an emerald, as yellow as a topaz, or as violet as an amethyst. Unlike minerals such as beryl or corundum that are a single species of stone with colored varieties, what we know of as garnet actually comprises several mineral species.

HISTORY AND LORE

The name garnet is possibly derived from the Latin *granatus*, meaning "grain-like," as it resembles the seeds of the pomegranate.

Aries, Leo, Virgo, and Aquarius

Because of garnet's color, suggestive of blood, it was once thought to make the wearer invulnerable to wounds, worn on the battlefield by both Christians and Muslims during the crusades. A protective stone, it was believed that garnets would turn dark when danger approached, resuming their original brilliance when the peril passed. According to Talmudic legend, a deep red garnet supplied the only light on Noah's Ark.

In Italy, garnets are traditionally associated with widows, who wear garnet beads in their necklaces and hairpins.

Mars

Some notable mining locations include India, Brazil, Australia, Russia, Tanzania, Madagascar, and the United States.

STRENGTHS

January

Garnet is an energetic stone that promotes passion, inspiration, and confidence. It is the gem of integration and regeneration, encouraging action and lending us drive, courage, and spontaneity. It stimulates self-awareness and encourages success, and is especially lucky when worn on a Tuesday. Garnet is thought to attract faithful friendship and affection. Keep one close whenever you need to lift your energy.

Root

HEMATITE

A powerfully grounding stone that transforms and releases negative energy and helps maintain one's sense of self.

PHYSICAL PROPERTIES

An opaque, steel-gray stone with a metallic to earthy luster. When polished, cut, or faceted, it shines like a mirror. Hematite is red when ground to powder: hence its name, which means "blood stone." Mars gets its red appearance from the presence of hematite on its surface, earning it its title as "the red planet."

HISTORY AND LORE

Aries and Scorpio

The ancient Egyptians carved hematite into headrest amulets, which were placed in tombs as both protective talismans and symbols of resurrection and rebirth. The ancient Romans associated the stone with Mars, the god of war – warriors used it on the field of battle to enhance courage and confer invulnerability.

In antiquity, the stone was thought to encourage prophetic dreams and, like obsidian, was used in the creation of scrying mirrors.

Mars

Some Indigenous American tribes used powdered hematite as a face paint before going into battle, as its bloody red color was thought to inspire courage in its wearer and fear in their enemies.

Hematite is found all over the world.

March and October

STRENGTHS

A stone that encourages victory in battles both internal and external, hematite stimulates clarity of spirit and strength of will. It is a deeply grounding stone that invites stability and encourages connection between the physical and spiritual planes. Contemplating its lustrous surface can be like gazing into a black mirror and can encourage revelations about our innermost selves. With a tendency to absorb energy, hematite can cleanse and recharge other stones.

Root

HERKIMER DIAMOND

A stone of clarity and introspection that aids in the discovery of self-knowledge.

PHYSICAL PROPERTIES

A clear and highly lustrous species of quartz, frequently doubly terminated: a rare trait among naturally occurring crystals.

HISTORY AND LORE

Sagittarius

So named due to its discovery in the Herkimer region of New York, the Herkimer diamond has also been called the "stone of attunement." Due to its double-terminated shape, it is often used by spiritual practitioners and sages as a pendulum to aid in rituals of healing and divination.

In the Feng Shui tradition, this stone is believed to disperse positive energy when placed in a window.

Uranus

The Herkimer diamond is found in and around Herkimer County and in the Mohawk River Valley in the United States.

STRENGTHS

April

The Herkimer diamond is an amplifying stone, known for attracting and heightening spiritual energy. It removes emotional or spiritual blockages and engenders harmony. The Herkimer diamond helps us see ourselves more clearly, encouraging us to accept and celebrate our individuality. It is considered a powerful dream stone, which may be used to focus the mind during meditation and enhance visualization, or be placed under the pillow to stimulate dreams and improve spiritual sight. Like clear quartz, it boosts the properties of other crystals.

Crown and Third Eye

ICELAND SPAR

A guiding stone that opens the way to your true path.

PHYSICAL PROPERTIES

A brittle, clear variety of calcite, sometimes with rainbow inclusions. Anything viewed through Iceland spar is seen as a double image, an effect known as birefringence.

HISTORY AND LORE

Cancer and Aquarius

Known as *silfurberg* (meaning "silver rock") in Iceland, this stone was once used by Vikings as a navigating tool because rays of light that enter the crystal become polarized and split, taking two paths to exit the crystal. This polarizing effect allowed Vikings to find the sun even in the densest fog, helping them navigate successfully when they would have otherwise been lost. Because of this, ancient texts refer to the crystal as a "sunstone."

Moon

The locality of Helgustaðir in Iceland was the primary source of the stone up until the early twentieth century; it was later discovered in other parts of the world including Mexico, Siberia, China, and Brazil.

STRENGTHS

June and July

Third Eye

Iceland spar is a meditative stone that clears the mind and increases concentration and motivation. Some specimens show beautiful iridescent dispersion which, when gazed upon, quells restless thoughts and encourages quiet contemplation. Iceland spar initiates transformation, transmuting negative energy and releasing it into the Earth to be neutralized. When faced with indecision, Iceland spar provides guidance and clarity toward a positive outcome. It resonates with those ruled by the sun.

IOLITE

A centering stone that encourages clarity, reflection, and deep thought.

PHYSICAL PROPERTIES

Ranges from blue to purple to violet to gray, with a vitreous luster. Iolite is particularly noted for its pleochroism, meaning it changes color depending on how light hits it – it appears intensely blue in one direction, yellowish-gray in another, and almost colorless in another.

HISTORY AND LORE

The word iolite comes from the Greek word *ios*, meaning "violet," and *lithos*, meaning "stone." Also known as a water sapphire, iolite was once believed to foretell storms by changing its hue.

Like Iceland spar and lodestone, iolite was used by early seafarers to aid navigation – owing to its pleochroism, the Vikings used iolite to determine the direction of the sun when it was behind thick clouds or below the horizon.

Iolite is considered to embody yin energy – quiet, reflective, and passive.

The crystal is mainly found in Sri Lanka, Africa, India, Brazil, and Norway.

STRENGTHS

Iolite is a stone for visionaries and leaders. It promotes clear thinking and intuition, and positively channels our influence on others. It is a stone of discernment that unlocks hidden regions of the subconscious to help us perceive truth – it allows us to ask, "Who am I when no one is watching?" Due to its chameleon-like quality, it is a useful stone to help shift perspective and gain insight into the thoughts and feelings of others who we may struggle to understand. Keep iolite close at night to aid sleep and unlock creative thought.

Aquarius

Saturn

January and February

Crown and Third Eye

JADEITE

This soothing stone imparts strength and encourages harmony in equal measure.

PHYSICAL PROPERTIES

A stone with a smooth, waxy surface and muted hue. Frequently green, it can also be yellow, rust red, or blue. Jadeite, along with nephrite, is commonly referred to as jade, but jadeite is harder, composed of interlocking blocky, granular crystals, while nephrite is fibrous.

HISTORY AND LORE

Humans have been using jadeite since at least the Neolithic period, when it was used to fashion axe heads and other tools. Thought to bridge the spiritual and material realms, jadeite was used by ancient Egyptians, Meso-Americans, and Chinese to protect the departed on their journey to the afterlife.

In China, jadeite has a long tradition as a stone of good fortune, held above all others. There, jadeite discs called bi have been carved since the Neolithic period; historians believe these ancient discs were symbols of heaven. The Māori of New Zealand also regard jadeite as sacred, using it in the creation of spiritually significant heirloom pendants known as hei-tiki.

Most jadeite comes from Myanmar, but it is also found in Russia, Japan, Guatemala, and the United States.

STRENGTHS

A stone associated with wisdom and tranquility, jadeite offers peace through strength and strength through peace. It has a stabilizing effect and encourages a healthy connection between body and mind. Jadeite brings harmony and a quiet joy up from the soul's depths, while encouraging tranquil energy in the body; it is well suited for use during meditation and relaxation. Considered particularly auspicious, jadeite invites happiness.

Libra

Venus and Neptune

March

Heart

JASPER

Inviting steadfastness and willpower, this stone links us to the body and the Earth.

PHYSICAL PROPERTIES

An opaque stone with boldly mottled colors ranging from yellow to green, red, brown, black, and gray.

HISTORY AND LORE

As jasper's markings were thought to resemble letters in the ancient world, it was considered the stone of Hermes and Thoth, gods of communication and knowledge in the Greek and Egyptian traditions respectively. In ancient India it was reputed to bring rain; this belief was also part of Indigenous American tradition.

In the European Middle Ages, it was a warrior's stone that was also thought to protect its wearer from snakebites, a belief dating back to at least the fourth century. In Italy, a piece of red jasper hung from a red ribbon was traditionally considered a powerful amulet against harm, while green jasper was reputed to ward off phantasms and witchcraft.

Jasper is found widely across the world.

STRENGTHS

An active stone symbolizing willpower, jasper lends drive and determination to all endeavors. It resonates with the physical body, lending a practical and grounding energy. It enhances concentration by keeping both mind and body anchored and promotes the flow of new ideas – ideas based in reality rather than mere fancies or fantasy. A useful talisman for inviting focus, stemming procrastination, and quieting a restless mind – use jasper as a touchstone when undertaking stressful mental tasks.

Leo

Mercury, Venus, Mars, and Jupiter

March

Root

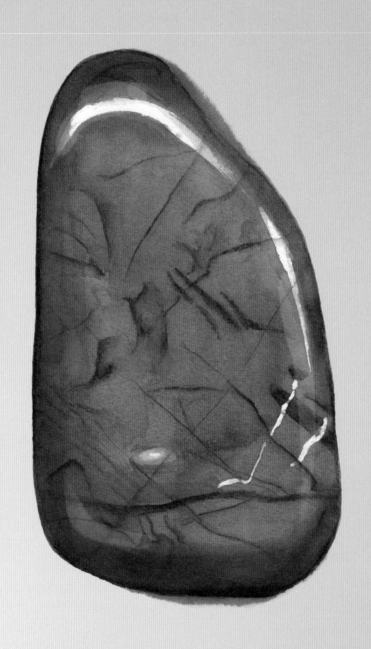

JET

With its purifying properties, jet is a powerful healer and agent of transformation.

PHYSICAL PROPERTIES

A lustrous, velvet-black stone that can be highly polished. Jet sometimes contains small pyrite inclusions that give it a metallic color. Jet is not technically a gem, but wood that has been buried for millions of years and compressed into a type of fossil.

HISTORY AND LORE

Capricorn

In ancient Greece, jet was considered sacred to Cybele, the wild goddess of mountains and caves, and was used as a protective badge for travelers. In England during the Middle Ages, it was often fashioned into rosaries, which were thought to banish the devil and other evil spirits. During this same period, it was burned in a similar fashion to incense, its smoke thought to drive off ghosts and demons; this tradition echoes the ancient Roman belief that jet's smoke drove off snakes.

Earth and Saturn

In the mid-nineteenth century, Queen Victoria adopted jet jewelry as part of her mourning costume after the death of her husband, Albert. The fashion for jet mourning jewelry soon spread throughout British society, and consequently, jet came to be associated with death and bereavement.

The most famous source of jet is Whitby in the United Kingdom, but it is also found across the United States, Spain, Turkey, Portugal, Italy, France, Canada, Cambodia, and Australia.

January

STRENGTHS

Third Eye and Root

Jet is a purifying stone, known to draw out negative energies, promote inner connection, and banish melancholy. It helps to uncover wounds carried in the subconscious, and works to neutralize them. Useful in times of hardship to promote healing. Jet can purify and cleanse other stones placed in a bowl with it.

LABRADORITE

A stone of transformation and transmutation, labradorite opens the mind to intuition and self-knowledge.

PHYSICAL PROPERTIES

Characterized by an iridescent play of color – blues, greens, reds, yellows, and golds – across a smoky gray backdrop, an effect known as labradorescence.

Aquarius

HISTORY AND LORE

Labradorite takes its name from its place of official discovery, when Moravian missionaries found it in 1770 on St Paul Island, off the coast of Labrador. Due to its relatively recent discovery, it has less associated superstitions than other stones.

Moon and Uranus

Labradorite is found in the United States, Canada, Madagascar, Russia, Norway, and the United Kingdom, while a rare variation called spectrolite – prized for its vivid colors encompassing the whole light spectrum – is found in Finland.

February and March

STRENGTHS

Labradorite is a stone of the spirit, fortifying the aura and providing protection against psychic disturbances. A talisman against depression and unhealthy thought patterns, it awakens joy and self-discovery, cleanses negative energy, and brings about spiritual rebirth. With its shimmering play of colors, this stone helps access different levels of energy and awareness, and has the capacity to help you realize untapped potentials. Labradorite lifts the consciousness and opens the soul to the magic of the everyday. Keep it close when embarking on a creative project.

Third Eye and Solar Plexus

LAPIS LAZULI

A tranquil stone of self-knowledge and reflection, lapis lazuli contains the mysterious beauty of the night sky.

PHYSICAL PROPERTIES

An opaque, deep blue stone, flecked with grains of bright gold pyrite. Lapis lazuli has a dull luster and is a variety of lazurite.

HISTORY AND LORE

Lapis lazuli takes its name from the Latin word *lapis*, meaning "stone," and the Persian words *lājevard* or *lāzaward*, meaning "sky" or "heavens." Sometimes called the "gem of the stars," lapis lazuli is associated with God in the Old Testament, regarded as a symbol of heaven because its appearance recalls both the blue of the sky and the gold of the stars scattered across it.

Aquarius

In ancient Egypt, it was seen as a symbol of truth and justice, associated with both Isis, goddess of healing and magic, and Maat, mother of truth, while the ancient Sumerians connected the stone with Inanna (known as Ishtar to the Assyrians), the goddess of love, war, and fertility. In the Buddhist tradition, the Blue Buddha, who protects from illness and misfortune (also known as the Buddha of Medicine or Healing) is represented by lapis lazuli.

Mercury,
Jupiter, Saturn,
and Neptune

The highest quality stones come from Afghanistan, but it is also found in Chile, Canada, Russia, Myanmar, and the United States.

STRENGTHS

December

Lapis lazuli is a stone of protection and tranquility, known to purge melancholy and fortify the heart. It is the stone of the spiritual seeker and the student, encouraging humility and self-knowledge. It helps release stress and encourages inner peace. A powerful talisman for bringing plans to fruition. Lapis lazuli is an excellent connector of heart and mind, helps in developing positive interpersonal relationships, and encourages interconnectedness between the inner world and the physical plane.

Third Eye

LODESTONE

A stone of uniquely magnetic properties that helps the wayfarer and spiritual seeker on their intended path.

PHYSICAL PROPERTIES

A black or brownish-black stone with a metallic luster. Lodestone is a kind of magnetite that has become naturally magnetized; when suspended on a string, a small piece of lodestone will align itself with Earth's magnetic field.

HISTORY AND LORE

According to one theory, the lodestone's name is a corruption of the Latin *Lydius lapis*, or "the stone of Lydia."

Scorpio

In ancient Greece, it was believed that when a lodestone was held against the head, one could hear the voices of the gods, gain heavenly knowledge, and see the divine. During the European Middle Ages, it was prized as a lover's charm, its magnetic quality thought to attract the affections of the beloved.

From approximately the twelfth century, it was used as the earliest form of compass by seafarers, who also carried the stone as protection against shipwrecks.

Mars and Saturn

Lodestone is found widely on Earth, and has also been discovered in meteorites.

STRENGTHS

October and November

Lodestone is a stone of reconciliation and love. It attracts positive energies and brings opposing forces into balance. Lodestone helps guide you when your path seems uncertain, offering clarity in times of confusion. It aids in finding one's place in the world, especially in regard to one's spiritual path. Keep a lodestone close when faced with a dilemma – with its dual positive and negative force, the lodestone offers a steadying and balancing influence.

Solar Plexus

It is said to be a fortunate stone for people with dark complexions, dark eyes, or dark hair.

MALACHITE

A stone of self-knowledge, understanding, and empathy, malachite offers abundance in all forms.

PHYSICAL PROPERTIES

A vivid and intense green stone with zones of light and dark tints that include shades of apple green, verdigris green, and emerald. Malachite is relatively fragile.

HISTORY AND LORE

The name malachite comes from the Greek word *malakee*, signifying the mallow plant, because the bright green of the stone recalls the color of mallow leaves. In ancient Rome, it was sometimes called the "peacock stone" and was considered the sacred emblem of Juno, queen of the gods.

Libra

According to folk superstition, heart-shaped malachite worn as an amulet will bring good luck in love. In Bavaria, malachite was once thought to bring good health to women, especially during pregnancy. A Russian legend has it that anyone who drinks from a malachite goblet will miraculously understand the language of animals.

Venus

Malachite is mainly found in the Democratic Republic of the Congo, as well as Australia, France, and the United States.

May

STRENGTHS

Malachite helps us to recognize and honor the highest good within ourselves, connecting us to life's sweetness. It assists in maintaining emotional balance and encourages a positive state of mind while guarding against the tendency to take on emotional burden from others. Malachite is a talisman of abundance, thought to multiply happiness, health, wealth, and love. A calming stone, keep one by your bedside to ward off insomnia and welcome restful sleep.

Heart and
Solar Plexus

MOONSTONE

A serene crystal, noted for its soft lunar glow and gentle, calming influence.

PHYSICAL PROPERTIES

A milky, bluish stone that appears to glow from within, with a mysterious appearance often likened to tears or raindrops. This shimmering, ethereal sheen is known as adularescence.

HISTORY AND LORE

Cancer

The ancient Romans believed the moonstone came from solidified rays of the moon, while it has historically been regarded as a stone for lovers in India. In medieval Europe, it was thought to cool heated imaginations and protect against moonstrokes and lunacy. During the Renaissance, moonstone was regarded as a powerful love charm during the moon's waxing; during the moon's waning, it would enable its wearer to foretell the future. During whichever phase, the stone was said to hold the radiance of moonlight and could thus banish nightmares.

Moon

STRENGTHS

June

Moonstone is associated with the nighttime, and all the mystery and romance that it brings. It enhances intuition and aids in receptivity and emotional awareness. It illuminates hidden truths that reside in the depths of our subconscious and brings them into the light, while connecting us with our feminine aspects. Moonstone is regarded as a talisman for the inward journey, and imparts a calm, centered energy during meditation. Kept under a pillow, it promotes restful sleep and wards off bad dreams. Moonstone is especially lucky when worn on a Monday.

Crown

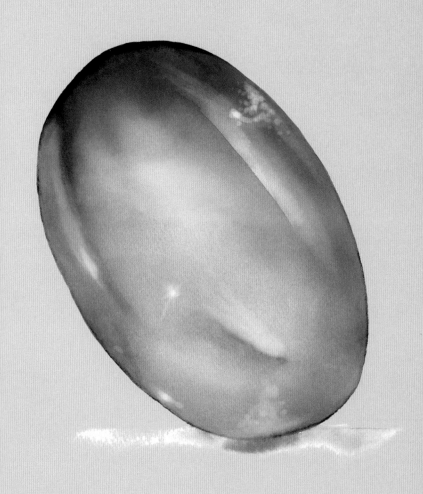

MOSS AGATE

A verdant, supportive stone that encourages positive growth and new beginnings.

PHYSICAL PROPERTIES

A green form of chalcedony with markings that resemble trees and vegetation. Stones that present with feather-like patterns are called plume agates, while those with tree-like, branching patterns are called dendritic agates.

HISTORY AND LORE

Taurus, Virgo, and Aquarius

Earth

June

Heart

In ancient Rome, moss agate was believed to bring prosperity to those who worked in nature; farmers would hang it from trees and around the horns of cattle to encourage successful harvests.

Moss agate was also sometimes used as a tool in water divining, and was thought, by ancient inhabitants of the Middle East, to control tempests and bring rain.

In the Victorian era, moss agate was a favored stone for mourning jewelry, its association with growth and verdancy symbolizing eternal life.

While moss agate is found all over the world, India is the leading source.

STRENGTHS

Symbolic of growth, moss agate is useful for stimulating transformation and aiding in transitions from one phase of life to the next. It encourages tranquility and emotional balance, and helps bring potential into its fullest flower, inviting feelings of expansion, freedom, and openness. Moss agate shifts all that is stagnant and brings about fresh growth. It encourages a connection with nature and helps us to access the sense of wonder and serenity we experience when surrounded by beautiful flora and vegetation – even when we're in an urban environment.

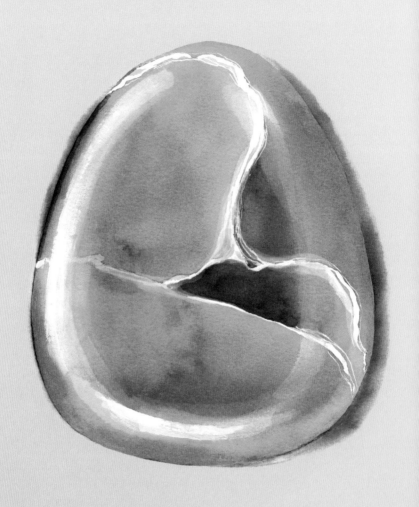

NEPHRITE

A stone of subtle strength, which opens the heart to renewal and abundance.

PHYSICAL PROPERTIES

A leek-green stone, sometimes found in blue, gray, and white, that is translucent to sub-translucent with a milky hue. Nephrite is one of two stones that is generally known as jade, the other being jadeite – of the two, nephrite is slightly softer and has a fibrous structure. One way to distinguish nephrite from jadeite is to tap the stone with a hard object – nephrite will chime with a musical note, while jadeite will not.

HISTORY AND LORE

Libra

Nephrite takes its name from the Greek *nephros*, meaning "kidney," due to a widespread belief that jade could cure kidney diseases.

As the difference between nephrite and jadeite wasn't discovered until around the eighteenth century, the two share a history and mythology; like jadeite, nephrite was thought to represent the nine accomplishments in ancient China: charity, goodness, virtue, knowledge, skill, morality, divination, rectitude, and harmony. It was sometimes called the "concentrated essence of love."

Venus and Neptune

Nephrite is most commonly found in New Zealand, where it is held sacred by the Māori, and is also found in Australia, Russia, China, Canada, Zimbabwe, and the United States.

March

STRENGTHS

Nephrite is a protective stone, symbolizing life, growth, and abundance. It encourages balance, even in times of stress or chaos. Nephrite soothes and harmonizes, and puts us in touch with our heart's wisdom. It suggests that strength can be found through vulnerability and openness – for this reason, it is helpful to keep close during times of emotional upheaval. It is thought to bring luck, especially in matters of love.

Heart

OBSIDIAN

Offering protection and encouraging powerful transformation, obsidian holds up a mirror to the soul.

PHYSICAL PROPERTIES

Glossy black or gray with an iridescent sheen and vitreous luster. Although typically dark and opaque, obsidian may also be transparent, and rare examples display chatoyancy (the distinctive ray of light seen in cat's-eye). Formed by the rapid cooling of volcanic lava, obsidian is not technically a gem, but a kind of glass.

HISTORY AND LORE

Scorpio and Aquarius

Obsidian was highly prized by ancient Meso-Americans, who called it *iztli* or *teotetl*, meaning "divine stone"; they used it in the production of weapons, mirrors, masks, and jewelry.

Like clear quartz, it was made into scrying glasses and used to divine the future throughout history – the famous astronomer, mathematician, and occultist Dr John Dee, advisor to Queen Elizabeth I, used an obsidian mirror to communicate with spirits.

Pluto

Obsidian is found in volcanic areas across the world.

STRENGTHS

January, November, and December

A powerful stone of protection, the obsidian offers a shield against negative forces while providing the means to confront the darkness within oneself. Obsidian helps uncover patterns of thought and behavior that may be inhibiting spiritual and personal growth, and offers the opportunity to let go of these unwanted habits. It promotes logical thought and helps to neutralize feelings of anxiety. Obsidian helps us come to terms with our shadow aspect and reminds us that something must end to make way for the new. Obsidian reflects truth and bolsters inner strength, welcoming spiritual cleansing and regeneration. It is especially lucky worn on a Saturday.

Root

OPAL

A stone of emotional, mental, and psychic harmony that encourages connection and deep insight.

PHYSICAL PROPERTIES

The white, black, or red of an opal is a backdrop to brilliant and varied flashes of red, blue, green, and yellow. All opals contain water.

HISTORY AND LORE

The word opal is derived either from the Sanskrit *upala* or the Latin *opalus*, both meaning "precious stone."

Leo, Libra, and Aquarius

In ancient Rome it was used as a curative stone for eye diseases, while also believed to open up the inner eye to receive visions. The Romans sometimes referred to opal as *Orphanus*, the orphan, because of its singular glory.

Opal is traditionally the stone of hermits and the gem of the gods who live alone, according to ancient Meso-American beliefs. Starting in the nineteenth century, it became unlucky in Europe and fell from favor, but this negative reputation has since faded.

Venus

Australia is the main source of opal, but it is also found in Ethiopia, Brazil, Mexico, Honduras, and the United States.

STRENGTHS

October

Opal represents ideals and their manifestation – a stone for leaders, creators, and artists. The opal aids focus, assisting meditation and encouraging creativity and inspiration. Few crystals are better suited to contemplation and meditation than the opal, on account of the beautiful array of colors held within its depths. Opal brings about both self-possession and self-knowledge: a powerful tool for encouraging inner strength and wisdom. It is especially lucky when worn on a Monday

Throat

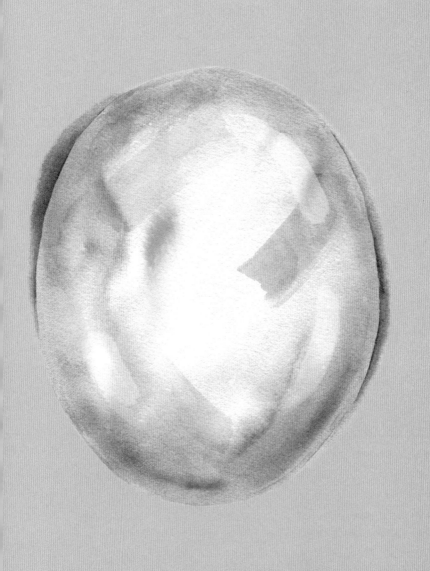

PEARL

A generative stone, recalling the beauty of the moon and the natural phases that shape our lives.

PHYSICAL PROPERTIES

Pearls are most often round, but can also be seed-like, pear-shaped, or irregular. In color, they range from white to cream, gray, bronze, rose, lavender, blue, yellow, orange–brown, and green, but all hues are delicate and elusive, with a luminescent sheen. The pearl is not technically a gem, but a dense shelly secretion that forms within some mollusks; as an organic material, pearls are very fragile and should be handled carefully.

HISTORY AND LORE

Cancer

The ancient Greeks thought pearls formed when lightning entered the sea, while the Romans suggested that they were the crystallized tears of water nymphs. Other ancient cultures believed that pearls were a combination of seawater and moonlight, and to this day, they retain their lunar association.

In Hindu mythology, different colored pearls have different associations: white is associated with idealism, black with philosophy, pink with beauty, red with health and energy, and gray with contemplation.

Moon

Pearls are found in coastal waters worldwide, although most modern pearls are cultured, rather than sourced in the wild.

STRENGTHS

June

Associated with the moon and the sea, pearl is symbolic of deep emotion and feminine power. It stimulates clarity and balance, especially in emotional matters – symbolically, it is a heart-opener. Pearl inspires healing and encourages emotional and spiritual transformation. Opening us to self-knowledge, it is a reminder of the natural cycles of things. Keep a pearl close whenever you feel alienated from your emotions to encourage a deeper connection with the self. Pearl is especially lucky when worn on a Monday.

Sacral

PERIDOT

Carrying with it vitalizing solar energy, the peridot is an uplifting and stabilizing stone.

PHYSICAL PROPERTIES

A stone with a yellowish green or bottle-green hue, with a vitreous to greasy luster. Under the right conditions, the stone can fall from the sky during volcanic eruptions.

HISTORY AND LORE

Leo

Sun, Venus, and Earth

August

Heart and Solar Plexus

Peridot is also known as olivine or chrysolite (derived from the Greek words *chrȳsos*, meaning "gold," and *lithos*, meaning "stone"). The ancient Greeks associated peridot with the sun, while the Romans referred to it as the "evening emerald" because it did not darken at night like emerald, still shimmering under candlelight. In fact, according to legend, it is impossible to find a peridot during the day because it would not reveal its true radiance until darkness fell. In Hawaiian mythology, peridots were thought to be the tears of Pele, the goddess of fire and volcanoes.

Peridot is found all over the world, with important deposits located in Australia, Brazil, Mexico, China, Pakistan, Sri Lanka, and the United States.

STRENGTHS

Peridot is a stone of stability, promoting reason, responsibility, and forgiveness. It enhances emotional strength and repels psychological disturbances. With its solar associations, it brings light to inner darkness and helps us see things with a positive perspective. Kept close at night, it wards off nightmares and sleeplessness.

CRYSTAL CLEAR

PYRITE

With its metallic glitter, pyrite sparks inspiration and helps cultivate inner fire.

PHYSICAL PROPERTIES

A brass-yellow mineral with a resplendent, metallic luster resembling polished steel. Pyrite is a common mineral, frequently mistaken for gold because of its glittering appearance – for this reason, it's sometimes called "fool's gold."

Leo and
Scorpio

HISTORY AND LORE

Pyrite's name is derived from the Greek *pyr* or *pyros*, meaning "fire," because pyrite emits sparks when struck, in the same manner as flint.

In England, pieces of pyrite were once known as "thunderbolts" and were thought to offer protection from storms and lightning – a long-standing folk belief which persisted until the nineteenth century. In Switzerland and France, pyrite was historically known as *pierre de santé*, meaning "health stone," as it was believed to grow pale if its wearer was about to become unwell.

Sun and
Mars

Pyrite is found worldwide, with important locations including Italy, China, Russia, and Peru.

July and
August

STRENGTHS

Pyrite is a stone for activity, inviting focus and encouraging determination. Its reflective qualities make it a useful stone to meditate with, as it invites fresh insights and encourages us to see things in a new light. Pyrite stimulates positive energy, sparks new ideas, and drives prosperity and achievement. It strengthens inner fire to help us fulfil our life's destiny.

Solar Plexus

CRYSTAL CLEAR

ROSE QUARTZ

An awakening stone that opens
the heart and soul to love in all forms,
and allows potential to blossom.

PHYSICAL PROPERTIES

Delicately pink in color and generally translucent, with an almost
greasy luster and milky appearance. Some rose quartz may display
a phenomenal effect called Tyndall scattering, which can make the
stone appear blue in certain light.

HISTORY AND LORE

Taurus and
Libra

Throughout history, rose quartz has been associated with feminine
energy and beauty; both the Egyptian goddess Isis and the Greek
goddess Aphrodite were believed to be intimately connected with
the stone.

Long used as a love amulet, rose quartz was also used during the
European Middle Ages for its healing properties. The poet William
Blake saw pink as the color of angels, an echo of the ongoing belief
that rose quartz brings spiritual happiness.

Venus

Rose quartz is found throughout the world, its most significant
sources in Brazil, Madagascar, South Africa, and India.

STRENGTHS

January and
February

Rose quartz is a stone of awakening, assisting with spiritual
attunement and welcoming compassion, tenderness, and
contentment. It invites love of all kinds, making its wearer both
more receptive to affection from others and open to embracing
self-acceptance. Rose quartz fosters inner potential, allowing
unrealized desires to unfold to their full beauty. It serves as
a reminder that the love we desire from others is already found
within ourselves. Keep one in your bathroom or near your vanity
to remind yourself of your inner beauty.

Heart

RUBY

A supportive stone that stimulates self-confidence, positive action, and the essential life force within.

PHYSICAL PROPERTIES

Rubies range from a delicate pink tint to pale rose red, true red, deep red, and blood red – the most sought-after shade is known as "pigeon's blood." Ruby is twin to the sapphire: they are the same mineral, corundum, differentiated by color.

HISTORY AND LORE

Ruby takes its name from the Latin word *rubeus*, meaning "red." Across the ancient world, it was associated with fire, and was thought to contain an internal heat that was capable of boiling water or melting wax.

Capricorn

The ancient Romans thought it combined *eros* (sensual love) and *agape* (spiritual love), and therefore represented the highest form of love. In ancient Myanmar, it was regarded as a sacred stone and was believed to represent a human soul in the last stage of transmigration before entering the eternal embrace of divine love.

Mars

In the eleventh century, it was believed that rubies originated from the heads of dragons and wyverns, a mythological connection that is echoed throughout history and continents. According to Arthurian legend, an enormous ruby atop the temple of the Holy Grail gave off light like a beacon, shining a path for the Grail knights to follow.

July and December

STRENGTHS

Ruby is a stone of power and action – it increases vigor and helps to overcome both inner and outer obstacles. It brings clarity, bravery, and positive energy, and is a powerful talisman against self-destructive thought patterns. The ruby stimulates the life force within, clearing out stagnant energy and encouraging passion in all its forms. It is especially lucky when worn on a Tuesday.

Root

RUTILATED QUARTZ

An amplifying stone, rutilated quartz inspires positivity, invigoration, and regeneration.

PHYSICAL PROPERTIES

A variety of transparent quartz with a vitreous luster, containing needle-like or hair-like threads of gold, silver, copper, red, or deep black.

HISTORY AND LORE

Sagittarius

Venus

Prized for its shimmering inclusions, rutilated quartz has gone by many names, including sagenite, *flèches d'amour* (love's arrows), Venus's hair stone, Thetis's hair stone, pencils of Venus, Cupid's arrows, Cupid's net, the goddess's tresses, and more. In ancient times, the threads of gold suspended in the crystal were thought to be beams of captured sunlight. It was used as a talisman throughout history for beauty, grace, skill in dancing, and ensuring the growth of beautiful hair.

This type of quartz is primarily found in Brazil and Madagascar, as well as Australia, Norway, Pakistan, Nepal, Mexico, and the United States.

STRENGTHS

July and August

Solar Plexus

Rutilated quartz is a high-energy stone with a revitalizing, purifying, and balancing effect. Known as an illuminator, it amplifies the properties of other stones and stimulates connection with universal energy. This stone encourages personal transformation and makes the mind receptive to a higher purpose and finding alignment with the truest self. Strengthening positive direction, rutilated quartz is like a shooting star – lighting the way to your true path. It is a lucky stone for those ruled by the sun.

SAPPHIRE

Symbolizing inner peace and spiritual attunement, the sapphire encourages an awakening of the spirit.

PHYSICAL PROPERTIES

Although it comes in many colors, sapphires are usually thought of as deep blue. The very darkest, almost black stones are called inky, while paler stones are sometimes called water sapphires. Sapphires are also found in shades of blue, violet, pink, white, green, black, yellow, and orange. Sapphire is twin to the ruby: they are the same mineral, corundum, differentiated by color.

HISTORY AND LORE

Taurus and Virgo

Sapphire takes its name from the Greek *sapphiros*, potentially originating with the Sanskrit *sanipriya*, or "beloved of Saturn." In ancient Persian mythology, the world was thought to rest on a giant sapphire, the reflection of which gave the sky its color.

Saturn

Churchmen in medieval Europe believed that sapphire could confer powers of prophecy on its wearer. The gem was thought to attract heavenly blessings to anyone fortunate enough to possess one – the clergy wore blue sapphires to symbolize their close relationship to Heaven.

Sapphires come from a variety of sources including Madagascar, Tanzania, Sri Lanka, Myanmar, and Australia.

September

STRENGTHS

Considered the gem of the soul, the sapphire is a stone of spiritual awakening and inner peace, encouraging devotion to higher purposes. This stone sharpens the mind and senses, and guards against melancholy. The sapphire will open barred doors and remove blockages in the spirit, and brings with it more peace than any other gem. Use a sapphire as an aid during prayer or meditation. It is a lucky stone for anyone born during fall.

Third Eye

SARDONYX

A stone of shielding and protection, sardonyx invites us to speak our truth without fear.

PHYSICAL PROPERTIES

An opaque, reddish-brown variety of onyx, consisting of sard and white chalcedony in alternate layers.

HISTORY AND LORE

Sardonyx's name is derived from the Greek *sarx*, meaning "flesh," because its color resembles skin. Unique among gemstones, sardonyx was thought to represent both the sun and the moon in the ancient Jewish tradition because of its red and white hues. The stone was highly prized by the ancient Romans, who used it to produce some of history's finest cameos, signets, and seals.

During the Renaissance, it was thought to confer eloquence upon its wearer and was highly prized by orators, lecturers, and elocutionists. The Swedish mystic and scientist Emanuel Swedenborg called sardonyx a symbol of "love of Good and Light."

Sardonyx primarily comes from Sri Lanka, as well as India, Uruguay, and Brazil.

STRENGTHS

A stone of strength and protection, sardonyx is associated with courage, wellbeing, and clear communication. It combines the stability and determination of carnelian with the focus and resilience of onyx, making it a stone that strengthens resolve and helps to maintain healthy boundaries. Sardonyx aids in clarity of thought and deed, and encourages us to freely speak our truth. Keep one on your person whenever you need to communicate clearly. It is especially lucky when worn on a Sunday.

Leo

Mars

August

Throat and Root

SELENITE

A stone of attunement and
focus, selenite invites us to see
the sacredness in all things.

PHYSICAL PROPERTIES

A transparent, fibrous, lustrous gypsum with a silky luster.
Selenite is a fragile stone and should be handled carefully.

HISTORY AND LORE

Selenite is named for its soft luster, suggestive of moonlight;
its name means "moonstone," derived from the Greek *selēnitēs*,
meaning "of the moon." Its name also recalls the ancient belief
that certain transparent crystals (including selenite, moonstone,
and colorless beryl and topaz) waxed and waned according to the
moon's phases. In some stories, this gem originated from the moon,
flung down to Earth by beings that one seventeenth-century writer
called Selenites or Lunary Men. During the Victorian era, selenite
was sometimes used by psychical researchers and occultists in
their experiments with the spirit world.

Cancer

Selenite is found worldwide, with important sources including
Morocco, Australia, Madagascar, Mexico, Brazil, and the
United States.

Moon

STRENGTHS

Selenite is a powerful focuser and magnifier, inviting gentle
self-examination without judgement. It attracts love and invites
harmony, especially in romantic relationships, and encourages
a slow and gradual flowering of the heart. Selenite enhances
the power of imagination and creativity, promotes tranquility,
and offers spiritual insight and rejuvenation. It cleanses and
amplifies the energies of other stones. It is a powerful crystal
for anyone ruled by the moon, and is especially lucky when
worn on a Monday.

June and
July

Crown

CRYSTAL CLEAR

SMOKY QUARTZ

A deeply protective stone that invites us to meet challenges with courage and fortitude.

PHYSICAL PROPERTIES

A transparent variety of quartz, ranging in color from smoky brown to gray to almost pure black, with a vitreous luster.

Scorpio

HISTORY AND LORE

The darkest varieties of smoky quartz are called morion, from the Latin *mormorion*, a name used by Pliny the Elder. Smoky quartz is the national gem of Scotland, where it is known as cairngorm, and has been highly prized since the time of the druids.

Mercury and Saturn

It was once associated with gods representing darkness such as the Greek Hecate, and was carried by warriors as a protective amulet, said to warn of danger by turning a darker color. In the European Middle Ages, it was carried in times of epidemics as a protective charm and placed on windowsills to discourage drifting spirits from entering.

September, October, and November

Smoky quartz is found all over the world, with major sources including Africa, Australia, and the United States.

STRENGTHS

Sacral

A physically and spiritually grounding stone, smoky quartz can shift stagnant energy and usher in new perspectives. It helps us become more embodied, more engaged, and more present in the world. Simultaneously, it reminds us that the only constant is change, and helps us to accept the inevitable ebbs and flows of life. Carry one with you in times of adversity to amplify your inner strength.

SUNSTONE

Representing light, warmth, and optimism, this stone reflects the energizing power of the sun.

PHYSICAL PROPERTIES

A transparent to translucent stone, with hues ranging from peach pink to bright orange and light red, with a vitreous luster. While most sunstones have inclusions of hematite or goethite, sunstones found in Oregon in the United States contain inclusions of glittering copper. Like labradorite, moonstone, and amazonite, the sunstone is a variety of feldspar, and is considered moonstone's twin. As a phenomenal stone, it exhibits a beautiful play of color when held in sunlight.

Leo and Libra

HISTORY AND LORE

Sunstone is named for its warm shades that glisten in light and recall the beautiful hues of a sunrise or sunset. Throughout history, it has been associated with solar gods, such as the Egyptian Ra and the Greek Helios, as well as with mythological heroes. To the native inhabitants of Oregon, the sunstone was formed from drops of blood of a great warrior, while in Canada, the stone was used in medicine wheel rituals.

Sunstone is found throughout the world, including India, Mexico, Norway, Russia, China, Canada, and the United States.

Sun

STRENGTHS

July, August, and September

A stone of creativity and purpose, the sunstone invites action, decision-making and the embrace of new opportunities. It reflects the positive, warm qualities of the sun, inviting openness, benevolence, and clarity. Sunstone helps us tap into inner reserves of determination and strength – for this reason, it is a helpful stone to keep close when undertaking exercise or personal training. It brings mind and body into alignment and stimulates passion, self-knowledge, and personal transformation.

Sacral

TIGER'S-EYE

A stone of integration and awareness that helps us let go of rigid thinking and appreciate the complexities of life.

PHYSICAL PROPERTIES

An opaque gold–yellow to red–brown stone with a silky luster. When the predominant color is a dark gray blue, it is known as blue tiger's-eye, hawk's-eye, or falcon's-eye.

HISTORY AND LORE

This stone was sometimes known as crocidolite, from the Greek *krókus*, meaning "the nap of woolen cloth," and *lithos*, meaning "stone," reflecting its silky appearance.

The ancient Egyptians believed that tiger's-eye represented divine vision and used the stone to decorate statues of gods. In ancient Rome, it was used as a protective stone by those going into battle. Tiger's-eye has been reputed to enhance the power of thought when held against the temple, and been used as a talisman against the Evil Eye.

Common sources of tiger's-eye include Australia, Myanmar, India, China, Korea, Namibia, South Africa, Spain, Brazil, Canada, and the United States.

STRENGTHS

Tiger's-eye carries the power of the sun, stimulating qualities of self-confidence, motivation, intelligence, and daring. It ushers in spiritual awakening and stirs thought into positive action – for this reason, it is a useful stone to keep close when experiencing mental fog or lack of concentration. With its alternating, shimmering bands of light and dark gold, tiger's-eye reminds us of the cycles of light and darkness in all things: day and night, summer and winter, life and death. Simultaneously, it helps us see beyond the world of dichotomies and encourages a harmonious understanding that all polarities are expressions of the single divine source of life.

Leo, Virgo, and Capricorn

Sun

July and August

Solar Plexus, Sacral, and Root

TOPAZ

A stone of powerful manifestation, topaz amplifies inner strength, determination, and confidence.

PHYSICAL PROPERTIES

Yellow is the color generally associated with topaz, ranging from amber to honey to straw yellow. Colorless topaz is the most common variety, however, and the stone may occur in almost any hue.

HISTORY AND LORE

Topaz takes its name from either the Greek *topazios*, meaning "to seek" or the Sanskrit *tapas*, meaning "heat" or "fire." The colorless variety is known as *pingos d'água* in Portuguese, and *gouttes d'eau* in French, both meaning "drops of water."

Sagittarius

Yellow topaz was associated with Ra in ancient Egypt and Apollo in ancient Greece, both sun gods. In the European Middle Ages, however, the moon was believed to directly influence topaz, increasing its powers for good as the moon waxed. It could function as both a sedative and a stimulant, according to the state of the moon. In legends, Saint Hildegard of Bingen was able to cure "dimness of vision" by lightly touching the eyelids with a topaz moistened in wine.

Mars

Brazil is the largest producer of topaz, but the stone is found throughout the world.

November

STRENGTHS

Topaz is a stone of influence and energy, aiding in creative endeavors of all kinds and helping to manifest goals. It encourages self-realization and regulates the emotions, encouraging us to let go of extremes and embrace a more balanced path. In its more passive aspect, it is a centering and grounding stone ideal for relaxation, meditation, and commitment. It is especially lucky when worn on a Sunday.

Solar Plexus

TOURMALINE

Showcasing almost all the colors on the light spectrum, tourmaline is a stone for expanding awareness and tapping into vital creativity.

PHYSICAL PROPERTIES

Tourmaline occurs in a breathtaking array of colors, including rubellite (pink, red), indicolite (blue), siberite (violet), verdelite (green), achroite (colorless), schorl (black), and watermelon (a bicolor stone of both green and pink). All varieties are pyro-electric – when cooled after being heated, tourmaline develops positive electricity at one end and negative electricity at the other, attracting dust, ash, and other light substances. For this reason, the Dutch called the stone *aschentrekker*, meaning "ash drawer."

Gemini

HISTORY AND LORE

In ancient China, red tourmaline was prized as a symbol of status, equal to the ruby.

Adherents of Hermetic philosophy in the early twentieth century associated tourmaline's ability to attract and repel with the caduceus staff of Hermes – itself representative of knowledge received and imparted. Like jet, black tourmaline was used almost exclusively in mourning jewelry during the Victorian era.

Venus, Saturn, and Pluto

Tourmaline is found widely, including in Australia, China, Pakistan, Afghanistan, Namibia, Brazil, and the United States.

STRENGTHS

October

A stone for creatives and intuitives, tourmaline is known for enhancing self-confidence and self-expression. It stimulates creativity and helps us think beyond the obvious, opening us up to new pathways and ways of being – keep one in your workspace when embarking on a new project. Tourmaline unites opposing forces and offers stability and understanding – use it to attract positive energy and exhilarate the spirit.

All

TURQUOISE

Representing wholeness, turquoise offers a protective, balancing energy.

PHYSICAL PROPERTIES

An opaque gemstone with a waxy luster. Most commonly robin's egg blue in color, it can also be sky blue, blue–green, or apple green.

HISTORY AND LORE

Turquoise is a French word meaning "Turkish stone," its name arising from the trade routes it took into Europe; in Türkiye, it is called *fayruz* or the "lucky stone."

To the ancient Egyptians, it was the sacred stone of Hathor, the goddess of the sky and universal mother. In ancient Tibet, it was associated with heaven, as its color reflected the blue of the sky, while it was considered a holy stone by many Indigenous tribes in the southwestern United States. The stone was highly prized by the Aztecs, who knew it as *chalchihuitl*.

Turquoise was considered a sympathetic stone during the Middle Ages in Europe, growing pale when its wearer was sick or unhappy. In both Eastern and Western traditions, it was believed that turquoise would bring happiness and good fortune if given by a loving hand.

Turquoise is widely found, with important locations including Iran, Egypt, China, India, Australia, and the United States.

STRENGTHS

Turquoise is a stone of protection and success, promoting wise counsel and good leadership. It supports internal balance and encourages clear communication, making it a useful stone in many spheres, including career, family, and relationships. Sometimes considered a bridge between the physical world and the spiritual one, turquoise helps us find a balance between creative impulse and practical considerations.

Sagittarius

Venus, Jupiter, and Saturn

December

Throat

Smith Street Books

Published in 2024 by Smith Street Books
Naarm (Melbourne) | Australia
smithstreetbooks.com

ISBN: 978-1-9230-4906-2

Smith Street Books respectfully acknowledges the Wurundjeri People of the Kulin Nation, who are the Traditional Owners of the land on which we work, and we pay our respects to their Elders past and present.

Publisher: Paul McNally
Editor: Avery Hayes
Design and layout: Vanessa Masci
Illustrations: Maya Beus
Proofreader: Pamela Dunne

Printed & bound in China by C&C Offset Printing Co., Ltd.

Book 309
10 9 8 7 6 5 4 3 2 1

MIX
Paper | Supporting responsible forestry
FSC® C008047